HOK SPORT + VENUE + EVENT

20 YEARS OF GREAT ARCHITECTURE

Editor: Patrick Bingham-Hall
Design: Felicity Hayward

Pesaro Publishing
PO Box 74
Balmain NSW 2041
Sydney Australia
Phone 61 2 9555 7422
Fax 61 2 9818 6999
Email pesaro@bigpond.net.au

HOK S + V + E (Firm).
HOK S + V + E : 20 years.

Includes index.
ISBN 1 877015 12 1.

1. HOK S + V + E (Firm). 2. Architecture, Modern - 20th
century. 3. Stadiums - Design and construction.
4. Auditoriums - Design and construction. I. Bingham-Hall,
Patrick. II. Title.

725

First Published in 2003 by
Pesaro Publishing, Sydney Australia

Photography © as credited
Text: © HOK S + V + E and Pesaro Publishing

Colour Origination by Universal Graphics, Singapore
Printed and Bound by Star Standard Industries, Singapore

HOK SPORT + VENUE + EVENT

20 YEARS OF GREAT ARCHITECTURE

20

COLLEAGUES, CLIENTS AND COMMUNITY

Telstra Stadium, Sydney, Australia during the XXVII Olympic Summer Games.

Great architecture evokes an emotional response; crowds united in purpose arouse a similar enthusiasm. The combination invites a particularly passionate reaction. Sports and convention facilities attract considerable attention in every corner of the globe.

The 1980s and 1990s have been an exceptionally eventful era for these facilities. Countless new stadiums, arenas and convention centres have been built, and hundreds more have been renovated. Many of those projects have emanated from a single firm: HOK Sport + Venue + Event. Its success has been forged with undeniable passion and tireless labour.

In 1983 five architects in Kansas City, Missouri, created HOK Sports Facilities Group, a design firm focused exclusively on sports facilities. That vision was echoed in London, England and Brisbane, Australia, where a practice called the LOBB Partnership had steadily evolved from a general practice firm into sport specialists. In 1998, the two came together to create the first truly global sports facility design firm, its three offices offering a uniquely fertile environment for pioneering design.

Its tradition of innovation includes the development of the club seating concept, which revolutionized the funding of sports facilities. In the early 1990s the firm's designers encouraged the idea of urban sports facilities and context-based architecture, inspiring a fundamental shift in stadium design. Its focus on sustainable architecture has led to continuous advancements, and many of its project designs have been honoured with the industry's highest awards.

Throughout the firm's evolution, its leaders have constantly explored new paths and new opportunities. Predicting that the focus on new sports facilities was slowly giving way to a broader marketplace, the firm's focus officially expanded to include convention centre design in 1996. A 2002 merger with Anderson Consulting Team, the pre-eminent leader in the world of special events, strengthened the presence in that industry. HOK Sport + Venue + Event was born.

On its 20th anniversary, HOK Sport + Venue + Event is focused on the future and poised for new successes. The firm employs 350 worldwide. Fourteen sport projects debuted in 2003, with three times as many on the drawing board. The Venue division earned a commission for their largest project ever, a major convention centre renovation. The Event division continued its efforts on various Olympic Games, all-star games and other events. With projects like the Nanjing Olympic Sports Centre in China, Wembley Stadium in England, and Phoenix Convention Centre in the United States, the firm is making a major impact on international architecture.

Each sports facility or convention centre represents a special opportunity to leave an enduring legacy, as these buildings become the public gathering spaces for each community. The firm's future rests on its continued ability to create extraordinary experiences for people. These buildings have ceased to be mere stadiums or convention centres, but have become destinations. HOK Sport + Venue + Event is devoted to designing the most spectacular buildings or experiences, the ones that set a team or a city apart. Their ultimate goal is to create places of magic.

伟大的建筑激发情感，有目的集会的人群产生类似的激情，两者结合唤起一种特别的激动。体育和会展中心建筑在全球的每个角落都非常引人注目。

二十世纪八十年代和九十年代是这类建筑硕果累累的时期。无数的新体育场，体育馆和会展中心落成，几百座完成扩建。其中有许多是 HOK Sport + Venue + Event 的作品。他们的成功是对建筑的热爱和日以继夜勤奋工作的结晶。

1983 年，密苏里州勘萨斯城的五位建筑师成立了 HOK 体育部，专门做体育建筑设计。同样的远见在英国伦敦和澳大利亚布里斯本得到共鸣-LOBB 公司从一家综合性建筑公司发展成专做体育建筑设计。1998 年，两家公司合并成为第一家真正的全球体育建筑设计公司，为在体育建筑上作前锋性设计提供了得天独厚的环境。

公司在设计上的革新包本俱乐部成员席概念的发展，从而改革了体育设施的资金来源。九十年代早期，公司的建筑设计师大力提倡市中心体育设施建设和尊重城市文脉，激发了体育场设计的根本改变。公司对可持续发展建筑的关注使建筑设计不断进步，许多项目赢得建筑界的最高奖。

在公司的发展过程中，领导者不断地探索新的道路和机会，预测将来新的体育设施会逐渐转向更广阔的市场前景，公司于 1996 年正式开发会展中心的设计市场。2002 年，又和世界赛事活动的领导者 Anderson 咨询公司合并，进一步加强了在同行业中的知名度，HOK Sport + Venue + Event 于是正式诞生了。

在这 20 周年纪念的日子里，HOK Sport + Venue + Event 全力为将来新的成功做好准备。公司在世界各地有 350 名雇员。2003 年新建了 14 座体育建筑，50 多个项目仍在设计中。Venue 部在做一个宏大的的会展中心的扩建。Event 部继续活跃在不同的奥运赛事、全明星比赛和其它体育活动中。项目包本中国南京的奥体中心、英国温伯尔登体育场、及美国凤凰城会展中心等，公司对国际建筑界产生巨大影响。

作为城市公共集会场所，每一座体育建筑或会展中心都是创造流芳百世作品的特殊机会。公司的将来着重于创造给人特殊体验的场所。这些建筑不再仅仅是体育场和会展中心，而更是吸引人的集会参观场所。HOK Sport + Venue + Event 将致力于为人们设计引人入胜的建筑和体验，从而创造出色的球队或城市。最终目标是创造一个富有魔力的场所。

Les grandes œuvres architecturales suscitent une émotion intense et les foules unies par un même dessein peuvent s'animer d'un enthousiasme comparable. Mais quand un public se rassemble dans un cadre architectural unique, son sentiment devient alors extraordinaire. C'est pourquoi l'érection de complexes sportifs ou de palais des congrès attire tant d'attention dans le monde entier.

Les années 80 et 90 ont été une période exceptionnelle dans ce secteur de la construction. Une multitude de stades et de centres de congrès sont sortis de terre, des centaines d'autres ont été rénovés. Nombre de ces projets ont été conçus par un seul et même acteur, HOK Sport + Venue + Event, une entreprise dont le succès s'explique par une indéniable passion et un rare goût du travail.

En 1983, cinq architectes de Kansas City (Missouri) fondent le HOK Sports Facilities Group, un bureau d'étude spécialisé exclusivement dans les installations sportives. En 1998, la société se rapproche de LOBB Partnership, un cabinet implanté à Londres (Royaume-Uni) et à Brisbane (Australie) et devenu progressivement un des experts de la conception de complexes sportifs. Une vision commune permet aux deux firmes de joindre leurs compétences et de créer ainsi le premier bureau d'étude de rang vraiment international spécialisé dans ce domaine. Sa présence sur trois continents va renforcer son esprit très innovateur.

HOK est à l'origine des abonnements privilégiés et des formules club qui ont révolutionné le financement des complexes sportifs. On lui doit aussi l'idée, datant du début des années 90, d'implanter ces complexes au sein des villes tout en respectant l'environnement urbain, ce qui a influencé de manière fondamentale la conception des stades. Sa défense de l'architecture durable a permis des progrès continuels et l'industrie a souvent reconnu l'excellence de ses projets en lui décernant ses prix les plus prestigieux.

Au fil des années, ses dirigeants ont constamment exploré de nouvelles voies et cherché de nouvelles opportunités. Prévoyant le ralentissement du marché des nouveaux complexes sportifs, ils ont lancé officiellement en 1996 un second bureau d'étude spécialisé dans la conception de centres de congrès. En 2002, la fusion avec Anderson Consulting Team, le leader mondial des manifestations spéciales, a permis de renforcer sa position dans ce secteur. De ce regroupement est née HOK Sport + Venue + Event.

A l'occasion de son 20ème anniversaire, HOK Sport + Venue + Event réaffirme ses ambitions pour le futur et entend bien continuer sur la voie du succès. La société emploie 350 personnes à travers le monde. Quatorze études de complexes sportifs ont été lancées en 2003 et le nombre total des projets en cours est trois fois supérieur. Pour sa part, la branche Venue Division s'est vu confier sa plus grosse commande jusqu'à ce jour avec la rénovation majeure d'un centre de congrès. De son côté, la branche Event Division poursuit ses activités pour les Jeux Olympiques, pour les matches des étoiles et pour la préparation d'autres évènements. Avec des projets comme ceux du Nanjing Olympic Sports Centre (Chine), du Wembley Stadium (Angleterre) et du Phoenix Convention Centre (Etats-Unis), HOK exerce un impact majeur sur la scène architecturale internationale.

Chaque complexe sportif ou chaque palais des congrès représente une occasion unique de changer le caractère d'une communauté de manière durable, d'autant plus que les foules se rassemblent sur ces lieux publics. L'avenir de HOK Sport + Venue + Event repose sur sa capacité à inventer des sites extraordinaires pour des expériences extraordinaires. Loin d'être de simples infrastructures, ses œuvres sont aussi des destinations. La firme a pour ambition de concevoir les bâtiments et les environnements les plus spectaculaires permettant à une ville ou à une équipe sportive de se distinguer. Son objectif ultime ? Créer des lieux à l'atmosphère magique. .

La arquitectura extraordinaria provoca reacciones emocionales; las multitudes unificadas con un mismo propósito manifiestan entusiasmos similares. La combinación de ambos elementos promueve reacciones apasionadas muy particulares. Los estadios, así como las instalaciones para la congregación pública provocan una considerable atención en cualquier lugar de la tierra.

Las décadas de los años 80 y 90 fueron una era de éxitos excepcionales para este tipo de construcción. Incontables nuevos estadios y centros de convenciones fueron construidos y centenares más fueron remodelados y renovados. Muchos de dichos proyectos tuvieron su origen en una sola compañía: HOK Sport + Venue + Event. Su éxito fue forjado con innegable pasión e incansable trabajo.

En 1983 cinco arquitectos de Kansas City, Missouri crearon HOK Sports Facilities Group, una firma diseñadora dedicada exclusivamente al desarrollo de instalaciones deportivas. Ese concepto tuvo similares repercusiones en Londres, Inglaterra y en Brisbane, Australia, donde un despacho con el nombre de Lobb Partnership evolucionó paulatinamente, hasta convertirse, de la práctica arquitectónica general, en una firma especializada en deportes. En 1998, ambas aunaron sus esfuerzos profesionales para crear la primera compañía de diseño de instalaciones deportivas con características verdaderamente globales, con tres oficinas en las que ofrecen

conceptos realmente singulares, con diseños de vanguardia.Su innovadora tradición incluye el desarrollo del concepto de club de butacas, el que revolucionó la financiación de las instalaciones deportivas. En la primera mitad de los 90 los diseñadores de la oficina fomentaron la idea de instalaciones deportivas en zonas urbanas y arquitectura basada en su contexto, inspirando un cambio fundamental en el diseño de estadios. Su enfoque en arquitectura sustentable promovió continuados desarrollos y a muchos de sus diseños les fueron otorgados los más destacados galardones de la industria.

Durante la evolución de la compañía, su directiva continuó explorando constantemente nuevas técnicas y oportunidades. Comprendiendo que el enfoque en nuevas instalaciones deportivas cedía lentamente ante las necesidades de un mercado cada vez más amplio, el enfoque de la compañía fue oficialmente expandido en 1996 para incluir diseños de centros de convenciones. La fusión en 2002 con la firma Anderson Consulting Team, preeminente precursor mundial en eventos especiales, fortaleció a la industria en ese campo. Así nació HOK Sport + Venue + Event.

En su vigésimo aniversario, HOK Sport + Venue + Event mira confiadamente hacia el futuro y está preparada para lograr nuevos éxitos. La firma emplea a 350 profesionales en todo el mundo. Catorce proyectos deportivos fueron inaugurados en

2003, con un triple más de proyectos en etapa de planificación. La división "Venue" ganó el contrato para el mayor proyecto en toda su historia profesional, la renovación de un centro de convenciones de gran envergadura. La división "Event" participó con sus esfuerzos profesionales en varios juegos olímpicos, juegos de estrellas y otros eventos. Con proyectos tales como el Centro Olímpico Deportivo de Nanjing, China, el estadio Wembley en Inglaterra y el Centro de Convenciones de la ciudad de Phoenix, en los Estados Unidos, la compañía imprime una indeleble marca en la arquitectura internacional.

Cada instalación deportiva o centro de convenciones representa una oportunidad especial para dejar un legado perdurable, conforme dichos edificios pasan a ser los espacios públicos de reunión de cada comunidad. El futuro de la firma estriba en su continuada capacidad para crear experiencias extraordinarias que puedan ser disfrutadas por el público. Estos edificios han dejado de ser simples estadios o centros de convenciones, para convertirse en especiales centros de atracción. HOK Sport + Venue + Event dedica sus esfuerzos profesionales al diseño de los edificios o de las experiencias más espectaculares, del tipo que distingue a un equipo o a una ciudad. Su objetivo más importante es la creación de lugares que dispongan de una magia especial.

Le opere architettoniche importanti evocano una risposta a livello emotivo; le folle unite per uno scopo comune suscitano un analogo entusiasmo. La combinazione di questi due elementi provoca una reazione particolarmente intensa. Per questo, i complessi sportivi e i centri congressi attraggono considerevole attenzione in ogni angolo del globo.

Gli anni ottanta e novanta sono stati un'epoca straordinariamente felice per questo tipo di strutture. Si è assistito alla costruzione di innumerevoli nuovi stadi, anfiteatri e centri congressi, e alla ristrutturazione di centinaia di altri. Molti di quei progetti sono stati il frutto di un'unica società: la HOK Sport + Venue + Event, il cui successo è stato forgiato con innegabile passione e impegno incessante.

Nel 1983 cinque architetti di Kansas City, Missouri, hanno creato l'HOK Sports Facilities Group, uno studio di architettura dedito esclusivamente alla progettazione di impianti sportivi. Quella visione ha poi raggiunto Londra e Brisbane, in Australia, dove una società chiamata LOBB Partnership si è trasformata gradualmente da studio con attività di progettazione generali a specialista in strutture sportive. Nel 1998, queste due entità si sono unite per dar vita alla prima società di progettazione di strutture sportive veramente globale, con tre sedi che offrono un ambiente straordinariamente fertile per la realizzazione di opere architettoniche di avanguardia.

Questa tradizione di innovazione include lo sviluppo del concetto della disposizione tipo "club" dei posti a sedere, che ha rivoluzionato il finanziamento dei complessi sportivi. Nei primi anni novanta, i progettisti della società hanno incoraggiato la realizzazione di strutture sportive nei centri urbani e un'architettura contestuale, ispirando un mutamento radicale nella progettazione degli stadi. L'interesse della società verso l'architettura sostenibile ha comportato avanzamenti continui, e molti dei suoi progetti sono stati premiati con i maggiori riconoscimenti del settore.

Nell'evolversi della società, i suoi leader non hanno mai smesso di esplorare nuovi percorsi e nuove opportunità. Partendo dal presupposto che l'interesse verso le strutture sportive avrebbe lentamente ceduto il passo ad un mercato più ampio, nel 1996 le attività della società si sono ufficialmente allargate abbracciando la progettazione di centri congressi. Nel 2002 una fusione con Anderson Consulting Team, il leader indiscusso nel settore degli eventi speciali, ha rafforzato la presenza della società in quel campo. È nata così la HOK Sport + Venue + Event.

Al suo ventesimo anniversario, la HOK Sport + Venue + Event è proiettata verso il futuro e pronta a mietere nuovi successi. La società conta 350 dipendenti in tutto il mondo. Quattordici impianti sportivi hanno visto la luce nel 2003, con tre volte tanti in fase di progettazione. La divisione Venue si è aggiudicata

la commessa per il progetto più ampio mai realizzato da questa divisione: la ristrutturazione di un importante centro congressi. La divisione Event ha mantenuto il suo coinvolgimento in diversi Giochi Olimpici, partite "all-star" ed altre manifestazioni. Con progetti come il Centro olimpico sportivo di Nanjing, in Cina, lo Stadio Wembley in Inghilterra e il Centro congressi di Phoenix negli Stati Uniti, la società sta avendo un impatto considerevole sull'architettura internazionale.

Ogni spazio sportivo o centro congressi rappresenta una speciale opportunità di lasciare un'eredità che dura nel tempo, poiché questi edifici diventano spazi pubblici di ritrovo per ciascuna comunità. Il futuro della società dipende dalla sua capacità di continuare a creare esperienze straordinarie per la gente. Questi edifici hanno cessato di essere semplici stadi o centri congressi, ma sono diventati vere e proprie destinazioni. La HOK Sport + Venue + Event mira a progettare gli edifici o le esperienze più spettacolari per contraddistinguere una squadra o una città. Il suo obiettivo indiscusso è quello di creare luoghi semplicemente magici.

Großartige Architektur löst eine emotionale Reaktion aus. In Menschenmengen, die durch ein gemeinsames Ziel vereint sind, kommt ein ähnlicher Enthusiasmus auf. Wenn diese beiden zusammentreffen, wird eine ganz besonders leidenschaftliche Reaktion hervorgerufen. Sport- und Kongresseinrichtungen finden in fast jedem Winkel der Welt große Beachtung.

Die 1980er und 1990er Jahre waren eine besonders ereignisreiche Zeit für diese Einrichtungen. Zahllose neue Stadien, Arenen und Kongresszentren wurden gebaut und Hunderte mehr wurden renoviert. Viele dieser Projekte gingen aus einer einzigen Firma hervor: HOK Sport + Venue + Event. Für den Erfolg dieser Firma waren eine ausgesprochene Leidenschaft und unermüdliche Arbeit verantwortlich.

Die HOK Sports Facilities Group, eine Designfirma, die sich ausschließlich auf Sporteinrichtungen konzentriert, wurde 1983 von fünf Architekten in Kansas City, Missouri, USA, gegründet. Ihre Vision wurde in London und im australischen Brisbane geteilt, wo sich eine Firma namens LOBB Partnership im Laufe der Zeit immer mehr von einer allgemeinen Designfirma zu einer auf Sport spezialisierten Firma entwickelt hatte. 1998 taten sich diese beiden zusammen, und es entstand die erste wirklich globale Designfirma für Sporteinrichtungen. Ihre drei Niederlassungen boten einen fruchtbaren Boden, auf dem Pionierarbeit in diesem Design-Bereich geleistet wurde.

Die Innovationstradition dieser Firma umfasste die Entwicklung des Konzepts von Clubsitzen, das die Finanzierung von Sporteinrichtungen revolutionierte. Anfang der 1990er Jahre förderten die Designer des Unternehmens das Konzept von städtischen Sporteinrichtungen und kontextbezogener Architektur, das einen grundlegenden Wandel im Stadiondesign inspirierte. Die Konzentration der Firma auf zukunftsfähige Architektur führte zu ständigen Verbesserungen, und viele ihrer Projektdesigns wurden mit den höchsten Auszeichnungen der Branche bedacht.

In der gesamten Geschichte der Firma haben ihre führenden Mitarbeiter ständig neue Wege erkundet und nach neuen Gelegenheiten Ausschau gehalten. Da sie voraussahen, dass der Fokus auf neue Sporteinrichtungen langsam aber sicher erweitert und auf einen breiteren Markt zugeschnitten werden musste, nahm die Firma im Jahre 1996 offiziell das Design von Kongresszentren mit in ihr Programm auf. Im Jahre 2002 erfolgte eine Fusion mit Anderson Consulting Team, dem überragenden, weltweit führenden Unternehmen im Bereich Special-Events, das die Präsenz der Firma in dieser Branche stärkte. Das war die Geburtsstunde von HOK Sport + Venue + Event.

Am 20. Jahrestag ihres Bestehens richtet HOK Sport + Venue + Event ihren Blick auf die Zukunft und ist für neue Erfolge bereit. Das Unternehmen beschäftigt weltweit 350 Mitarbeiter.

Im Jahre 2003 wurden vierzehn neue Sportprojekte eingeweiht und die dreifache Anzahl an Projekten befindet sich im Entwurf. Der Geschäftsbereich Venue verdiente sich eine Provision für ihr größtes Projekt aller Zeiten: die Renovierung eines großen Kongresszentrums. Der Geschäftsbereich Event setzte seine Anstrengungen bei verschiedenen Olympischen Spielen, All-Star-Games und sonstigen Veranstaltungen fort. Mit Projekten wie dem Nanjing Sports Center in China, dem Wembley-Stadion in England und dem Phoenix Convention Center in den Vereinigten Staaten hat die Firma einen bedeutenden Einfluss auf die internationale Architektur ausgeübt.

Jede Sporteinrichtung und jedes Kongresszentrum stellt eine besondere Gelegenheit dar, ein dauerhaftes Vermächtnis zu hinterlassen, denn diese Gebäude stellen in jeder Gemeinschaft öffentliche Versammlungsorte dar. Die Zukunft unserer Firma liegt in ihrer fortgesetzten Fähigkeit begründet, außergewöhnliche Erfahrungen für die Menschen zu ermöglichen. Diese Gebäude werden nicht mehr als reine Sportstadien oder Kongresszentren angesehen, sondern sind zu Erlebnissen geworden. HOK Sport + Venue + Event widmet seine gesamte Aufmerksamkeit dem Design der spektakulärsten Gebäude und Erlebnisse – von einer Art, dass sie ein Team oder eine Stadt von anderen absetzen. Das höchste Ziel von HOK Sport + Venue + Event ist, magische Orte zu kreieren.

Contents

Ascot Racecourse

Ascot UK

Year of Completion 2006

Arsenal Stadium

Ashburton Grove London UK

Year of Completion 2006

The Arena at the Millennium Dome

Greenwich London UK

Year of Completion 2007

Wembley National Stadium

Wembley London UK

Year of Completion 2006

Melbourne Cricket Ground Redevelopment

Melbourne Victoria Australia

Year of Completion 2006

(designed by HOK S+V+E as part of the MCG5 Joint Venture)

Nanjing Olympic Sports Centre

Nanjing People's Republic of China

Year of Completion 2005

Jacobs Field
Cleveland Ohio USA

Opened 1994 | Seats 43,348 | Club Seats 2,400 | Suites 125

Cleveland Browns Stadium

Cleveland Ohio USA

Opened 1999 | Seats 73,200 | Club Seats 8,754 | Suites 147

Durham Bulls Athletic Park

Durham North Carolina USA

Opened 1995 | Seats 10,000 | Suites 11

Franklin Covey Field

Salt Lake City Utah USA

Opened 1994 | Seats 15,500 | Suites 23

Dunn Tire Park

Buffalo New York USA

Opened 1988 | Seats 20,567 | Club Seats 2,665 | Suites 40

Alltel Stadium

Jacksonville Florida USA

Opened 1996 | Seats 76,000 | Club Seats 11,200 | Suites 90

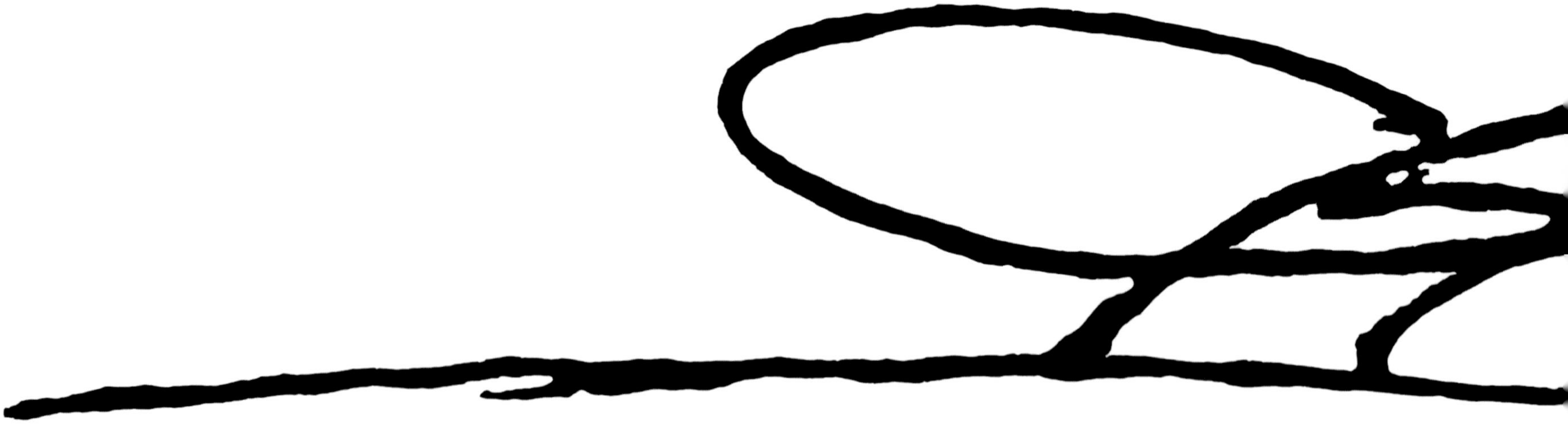

Bradley Center

Milwaukee Wisconsin USA

Opened 1988 | **Seats** 20,000 | **Suites** 68

Alfred McAlpine Stadium

Huddersfield England UK

Opened 1993 | Seats 24,500 | Suites 42

Cheltenham Racecourse

Cheltenham England UK

Opened 1997 | Seats 50,000 | Suites 10

Millennium Stadium

Cardiff Wales UK

Opened 1999 | **Seats** 75,000

University of Wisconsin
The Kohl Center

Madison Wisconsin USA

Opened 1998 | Seats 17,142 | Suites 36

Reebok Stadium

Bolton England UK

Opened 1997 | Seats 28,000

FedExField

Landover Maryland USA

Opened 1997 | **Seats** 86,484 | **Club Seats** 15,044 | **Suites** 280

University of Arkansas
Baum Stadium at George Cole Field

Fayetteville Arkansas USA

Opened 1996 | Seats 3,300 | Club Seats 88 | Suites 2

Victory Field

Indianapolis Indiana USA

Opened 1996 | **Seats** 13,500 | **Suites** 28

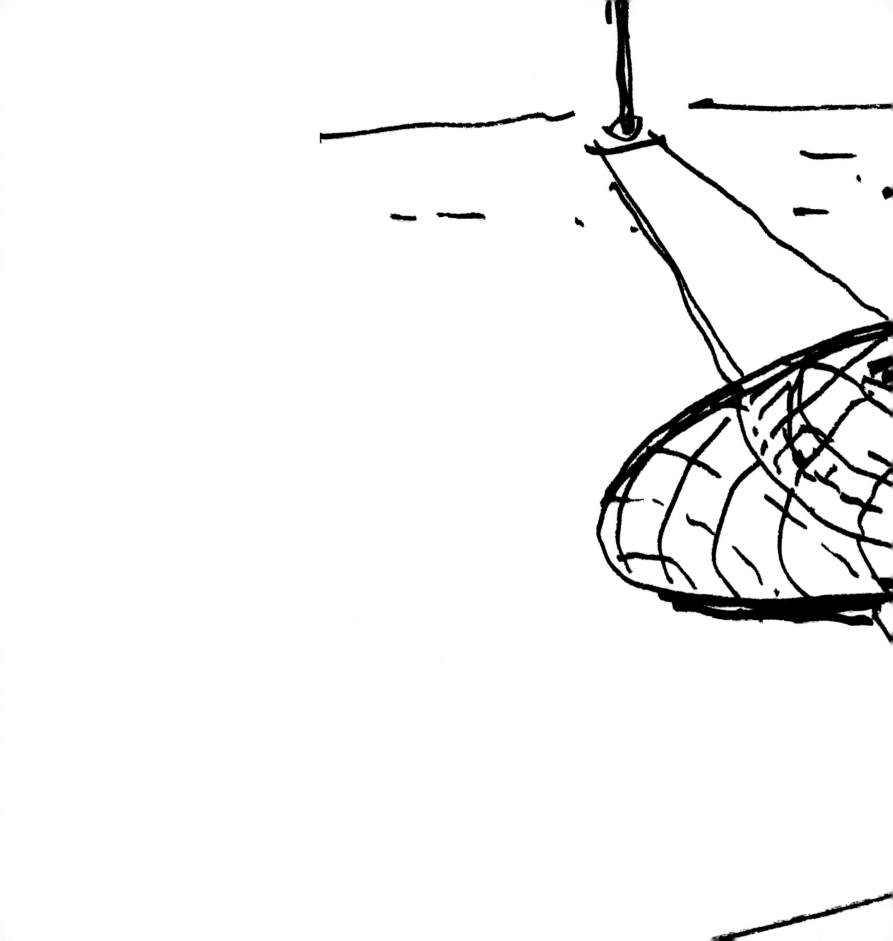

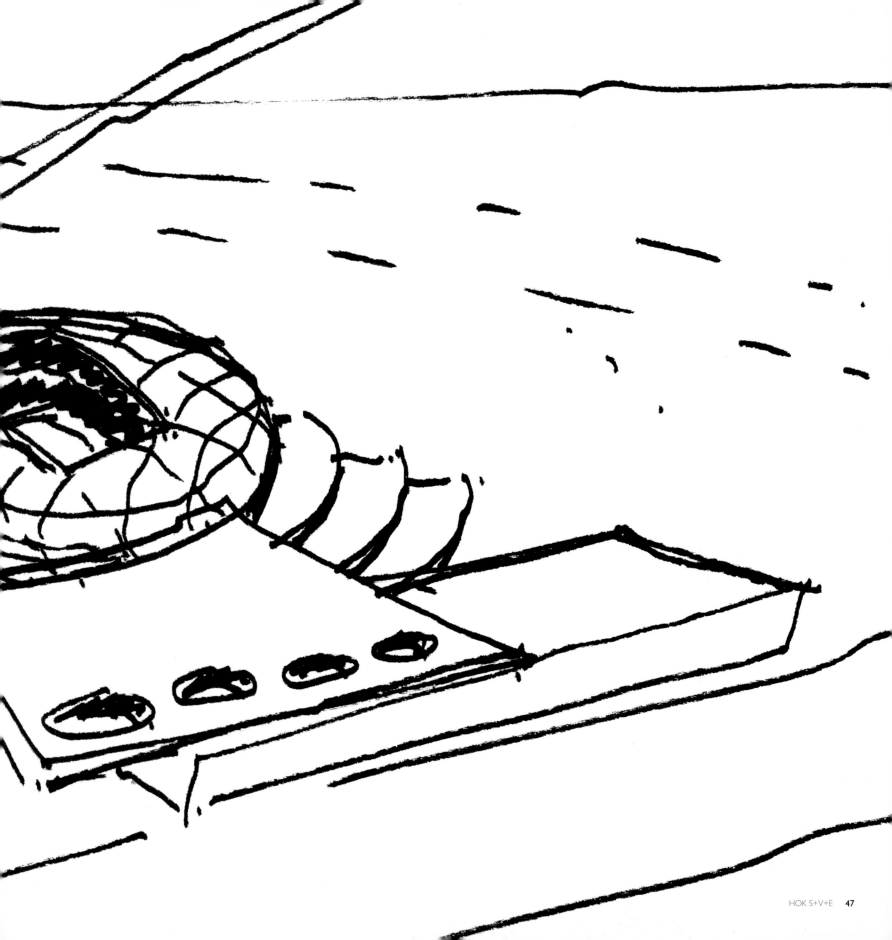

Suncorp Stadium

Brisbane Australia

Opened 2003 | **Seats** 52,500 | **Club Seats** 3,000 | **Suites** 72

Suncorp Stadium at Lang Park was designed by HOK Sport + Venue + Event, in association with PDT Architects

Hohokam Stadium

Mesa Arizona USA

Opened 1997 | **Seats** 12,500

Tucson Electric Park

Tucson Arizona USA

Opened 1998 | Seats 11,500 | Club Seats 469 | Suites 8

The Alamodome

San Antonio Texas USA

Opened 1993 | Seats 65,000 | Club Seats 7,000 | Suites 36

Harbor Park

Norfolk Virginia USA

Opened 1993 | Seats 12,067 | Club Seats 250 | Suites 20

Mile High Stadium Suites

Denver Colorado USA

Opened 1986 | Suites 60

Great American Ball Park

Cincinnati Ohio USA

Opened 2003 | Seats 42,059 | Club Seats 4,317 | Suites 61

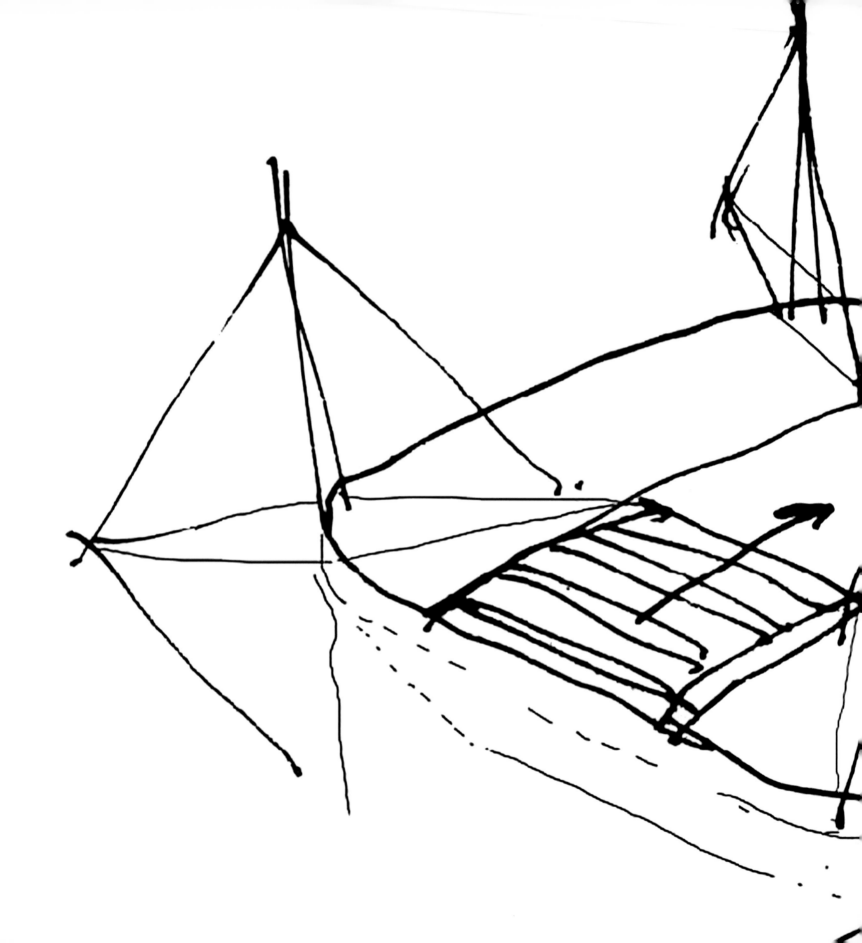

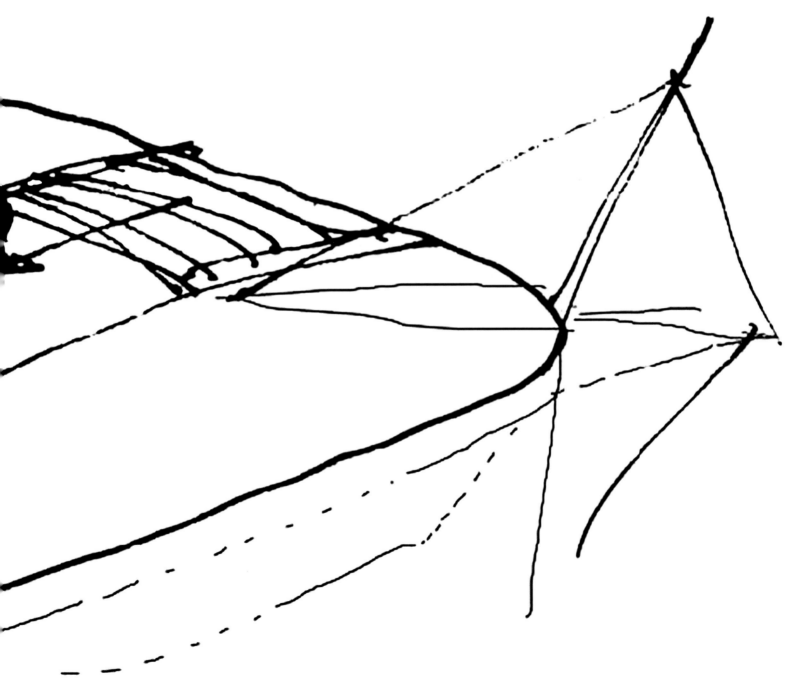

Oriole Park at Camden Yards

Baltimore Maryland USA

Opened 1992 | Seats 48,876 | Club Seats 5,125 | Suites 75

The United Center

Chicago Illinois USA

Opened 1994 | Seats 21,500 | Club Seats 3,100 | Suites 216

Xcel Energy Center

St. Paul Minnesota USA

Opened 2000 | **Seats** 18,064 | **Club Seats** 3,000 | **Suites** 74

Hallam FM Arena

Sheffield England UK

Opened 1991 | Seats 12,500 | Club Seats 100 | Suites 32

National Indoor Arena

Birmingham England UK

Opened 1991 | Seats 13,000 | Suites 14

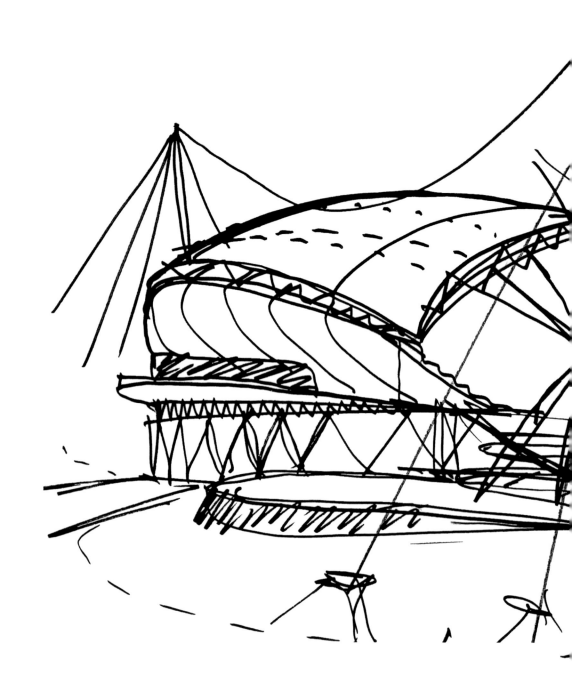

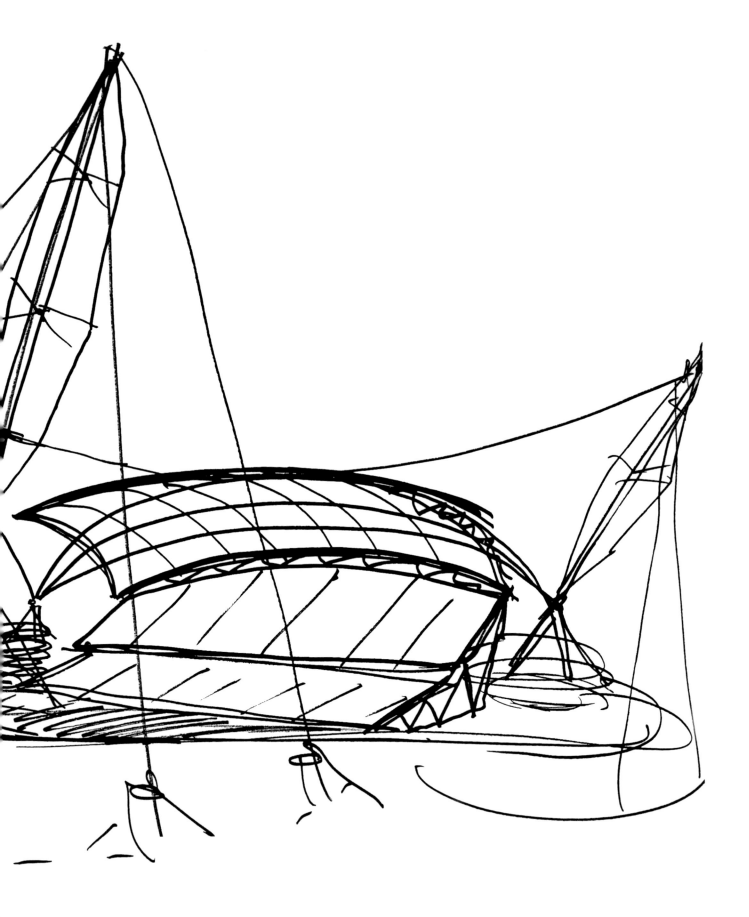

Hong Kong Stadium

So Kon Po Hong Kong China

Opened 1994 | Seats 40,000 | Club Seats 3,153 | Suites 50

Pro Player Stadium

Miami Florida USA

Opened 1987 | Seats 75,540 | Club Seats 10,200 | Suites 183

PNC Park

Pittsburgh Pennsylvania USA

Opened 2001 | Seats 38,365 | Club Seats 3,297 | Suites 69

Arrowhead Pond of Anaheim

Anaheim California USA

Opened 1993 | Seats 19,400 | Club Seats 1,720 | Suites 83

Homestead Sports Complex

Homestead Florida USA

Opened 1991 | Seats 6,500 | Suites 21

Stadium of

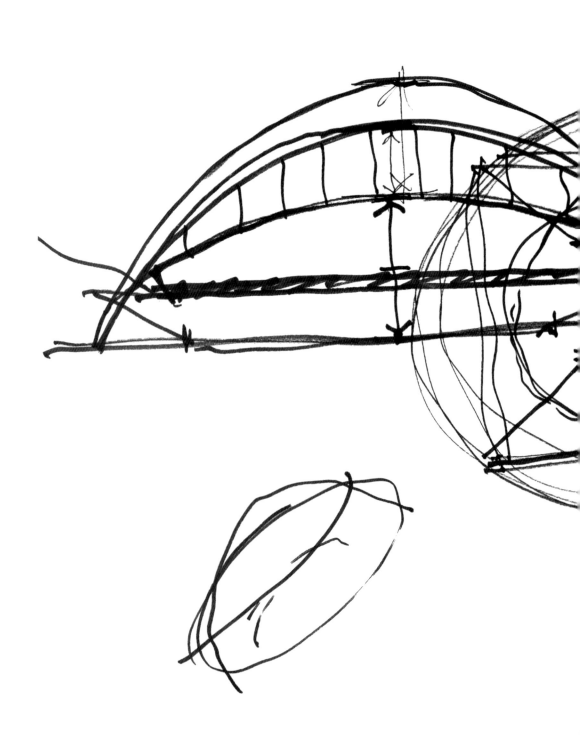

light

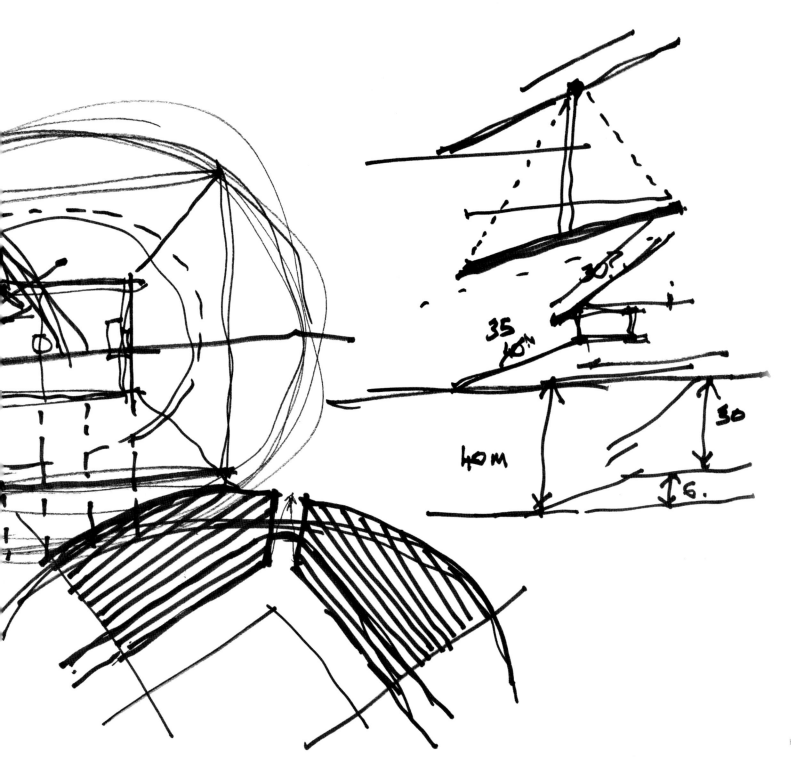

Philips Arena

Atlanta Georgia USA

Opened 1999 | Seats 21,000 | Club Seats 1,866 | Suites 92

The E Center

West Valley City Utah USA

Opened 1997 | Seats 12,000 | Club Seats 1,750 | Suites 50

Penn State University
Louis E. Lasch Football Training Facility

University Park Pennsylvania USA

Opened 1999

Gillette Stadium

Foxborough Massachusetts USA

Opened 2002 | Seats 68,000 | Club Seats 6,000 | Suites 80

Giant Center

Hershey Pennsylvania USA

Opened 2002 | **Seats** 12,500 | **Club Seats** 688 | **Suites** 40

Grizzlies Stadium

Fresno California USA

Opened 2002 | **Seats** 12,500 | **Club Seats** 600 | **Suites** 32

City of Palms Park

Fort Myers Florida USA

Opened 1993 | Seats 6,990

America's Center

St. Louis Missouri USA

Opened 1995

Telstra Dome

Melbourne Australia

Opened 2000 | **Seats** 54,000 | **Club Seats** 11,800 | **Suites** 67

Telstra Dome - formerly Colonial Stadium, was designed by an HOK Sport + Venue + Event joint venture, Bligh Lobb Sports Architecture and Daryl Jackson Pty Ltd. HOK Sport + Venue + Event is an HOK Sport subsidiary.

M&T Bank Stadium

Baltimore Maryland USA

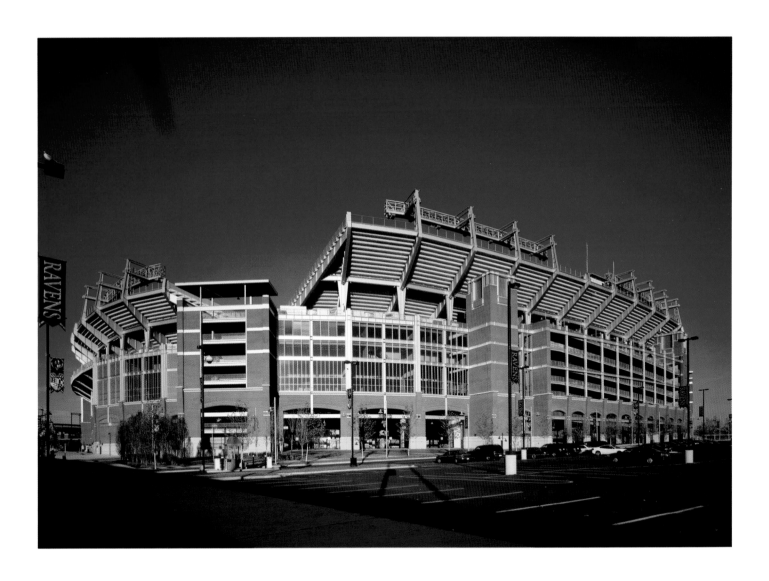

Opened 1998 | Seats 68,915 | Club Seats 7,904 | Suites 108

Joseph P. Riley Jr. Park

Charleston South Carolina USA

Opened 1997 | **Seats** 5,800 | **Suites** 8

Roger Dean Stadium

Opened 1998 | **Seats** 6,600 | **Suites** 6

Edison International Field

Anaheim California USA

Opened 1998 | Seats 45,030 | Club Seats 5,111 | Suites 78

Richmond County Bank Ballpark at St. George Station

Staten Island New York USA

Opened 2001 | **Seats** 6,886 | **Suites** 19

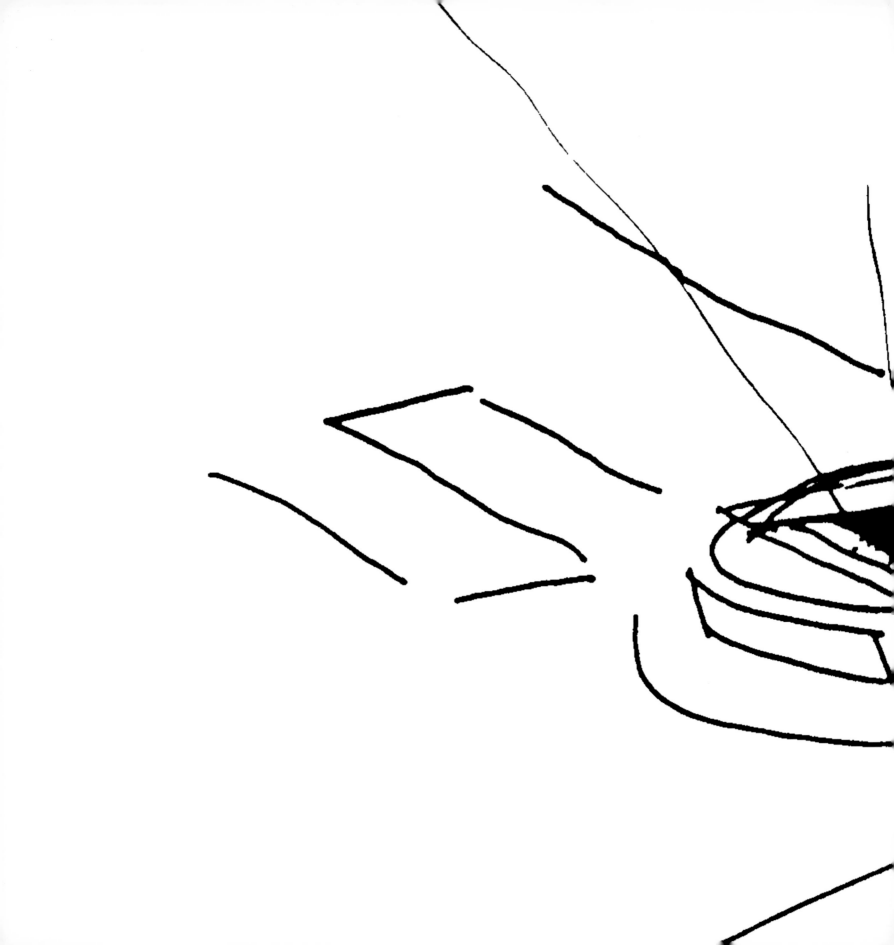

Reliant Stadium

Houston Texas USA

Opened 2002 | Seats 69,500 | Club Seats 8,200 | Suites 154

Pennsylvania State University
Beaver Stadium Expansion

University Park Pennsylvania USA

Opened 2001 | **Seats** 107,282 | **Club Seats** 4,000 | **Suites** 60

Stamford Bridge North Stand

London England UK

Opened 1994 | Seats 10,000

Minute Maid Park

Houston Texas USA

Opened 2000 | Seats 40,950 | Club Seats 4,776 | Suites 63

The Marie P. DeBartolo Sports Center

San Francisco California USA

Opened 1988

Fort Worth Convention Center Expansion

Fort Worth Texas USA

Opened 2003

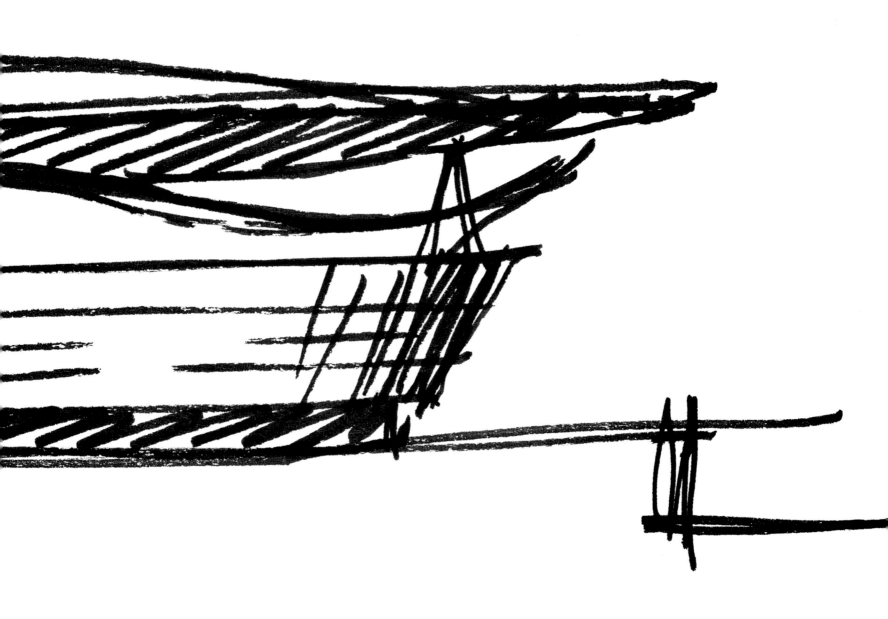

Anaheim Convention Center Expansion

Anaheim California USA

Opened 2001

The Baseball Grounds of Jacksonville

Jacksonville Florida USA

Opened 2003 | Seats 10,000 | Suites 12

Virginia Tech
Lane Stadium Expansion

Blacksburg Virginia USA

Opened 2002 | **Seats** 65,115 | **Club Seats** 1,202 | **Suites** 15

15th FIFA World Cup

USA

Opened 1994

Super Bowl XXXVII

San Diego California USA

Opened 2003

Telstra Stadium

Sydney Australia

Opened 1999 | **Seats** 110,000

Telstra Stadium - formerly Stadium Australia, was designed by an HOK Sport + Venue + Event joint venture, Bligh Lobb Sports Architecture

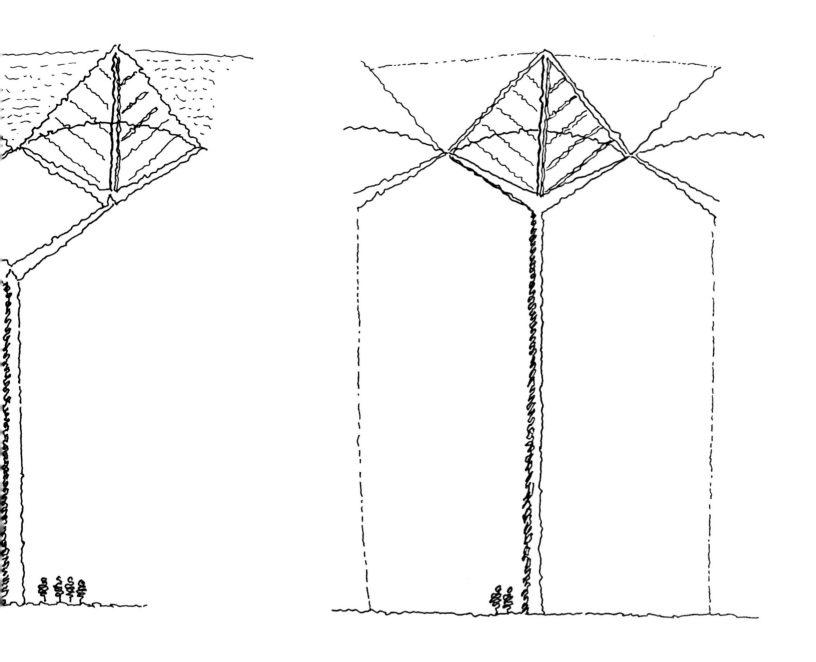

Opened 2002

XXVII Olympic Summer Games

Sydney Australia

Opened 2000

Sydney 2000 Olympic Overlay was designed by an HOK Sport + Venue + Event joint venture, Bligh Lobb Sports Architecture

Surprise Recreation Campus

Surprise Arizona USA

Opened 2003 | **Seats** 10,500 | **Club Seats** 500 | **Suites** 6

Scottsdale Stadium

Scottsdale Arizona USA

Opened 1992 | **Seats** 7,188

Indiana Convention Center Expansion

Indianapolis Indiana USA

Opened 2001

Wrigley Field Improvements

Chicago Illinois USA

Opened 1989

Heinz Field

Pittsburgh Pennsylvania USA

Opened 2001 | **Seats** 64,450 | **Club Seats** 6,600 | **Suites** 127

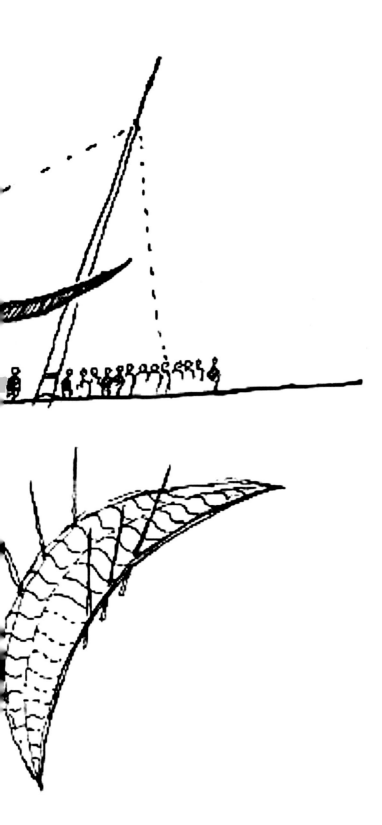

AutoZone Park

Memphis Tennessee USA

Opened 2000 | **Seats** 14,320 | **Club Seats** 1,500 | **Suites** 48

Isotopes Park

Albuquerque New Mexico USA

Opened 2003 | Seats 11,124 | Club Seats 709 | Suites 30

Ericsson Stadium

Charlotte North Carolina USA

Opened 1996 | Seats 73,258 | Club Seats 11,249 | Suites 158

John O'Donnell Stadium Renovation

Davenport Iowa USA

Opened 1989/2003 | **Seats** 5,200 | **Club Seats** 150 | **Suites** 20

University of Rhode Island
The Thomas M. Ryan Center

Kingston Rhode Island USA

Opened 2002 | **Seats** 7,700 | **Club Seats** 500 | **Suites** 8

Pepsi Center

Denver Colorado USA

Opened 1999 | Seats 20,000 | Club Seats 1,900 | Suites 95

TICKET SALES
WILL CALL

University of Kansas
Anderson Family Strength and Conditioning Center

Lawrence Kansas USA

Opened 2003

University of Houston
Athletics and Alumni Center

Houston Texas USA

Opened 1995

University of Tulsa
Donald W. Reynolds Center

Tulsa Oklahoma USA

Opened 1998 | **Seats** 8,355

Kansas State University
Wagner Field Expansion

Manhattan Kansas USA

Opened 1999 | Seats 50,300 | Suites 31

Gaylord Entertainment Center

Nashville Tennessee USA

Opened 1996 | Seats 20,000 | Club Seats 2,000 | Suites 72

XXVI Olympic Summer Games

Atlanta Georgia USA

Opened 1996

3rd FIFA Women's World Cup

USA

Opened 1999

University of Delaware
Bob Carpenter Convocation Center

Newark Delaware USA

Opened 1992 | Seats 5,000

Canal Park

Akron Ohio USA

Opened 1997 | Seats 9,097 | Suites 25

Coors Field

Denver Colorado USA

Opened 1995 | **Seats** 50,445 | **Club Seats** 4,500 | **Suites** 63

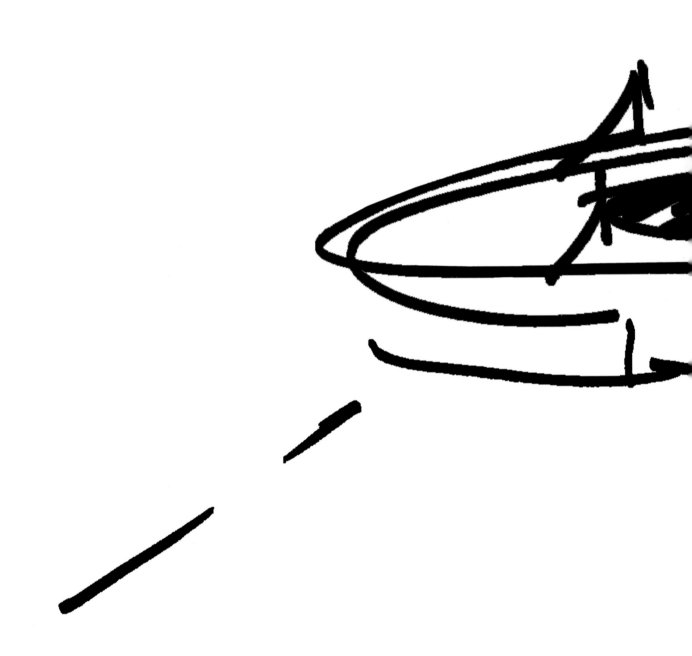

Westpac Stadium

Wellington New Zealand

Opened 2000 | **Seats** 34,500

Westpac Stadium - formerly Westpac Trust Stadium, was designed by an HOK Sport + Venue + Event joint venture,

Bligh Lobb Sports Architecture, in association with Architecture Warren and Mahoney

Comerica Park

Detroit Michigan USA

Opened 2000 | **Seats** 40,000 | **Club Seats** 1,000 | **Suites** 105

Pacific Bell Park

San Francisco California USA

Opened 2000 | Seats 40,930 | Club Seats 5,300 | Suites 67

Built Facilities, Renovations and Events

1986 National Basketball Association
All-Star Game
1988 National Collegiate Athletic Association
Men's Basketball Final Four
1989 Major League Baseball World Series
1990 Goodwill Games
1991 World University Games
1993 National Collegiate Athletic Association
Men's Basketball Final Four Consulting
1993 World University Games
1994 Federation Internationale de Football
Association World Cup
1996 Democratic National Convention
1996 Major League Soccer Inaugural Game
1996 Paralympic Games
1998 Asian Games Bid for Bangkok, Thailand
1998 Asian Games Bid for Taipei, Taiwan
1998 Confederation of North, Central
American and Caribbean Association
Football Gold Cup
1998 Federation Internationale de Football
Association World Cup
1998 National Collegiate Athletic Association
Women's Basketball Final Four
1999 Federation Internationale de Football
Association Women's World Cup
1999 Federation Internationale de Football
Association World All-Star Game
1999 Major League Baseball All-Star Game
2001 Goodwill Games
2002 Commonwealth Games
2002 Federation Internationale de Football
Association World Cup
2003 Major League Baseball All-Star Game
Aintree Racecourse
Air Canada Centre
Alfred McAlpine Stadium
All England Lawn Tennis Croquet Club
Improvements
Alltel Stadium
Alltel Stadium Club Improvements
America's Center
Anaheim Convention Center Expansion
Arizona State University Skybox and
Press Addition
Arrowhead Pond
Arrowhead Stadium Improvements
Arsenal Football Club North Stand
at Highbury Stadium
Arsenal Football Club Stadium at
Ashburton Grove

Ascot Racecourse Redevelopment
Augustana College Baseball Facility
Augustana College Ericsson Field Turf
Replacement
Autozone Park
Bakersfield Ballpark
Baseball City Spring Training Facility
Benfica Stadium
Bradley Center
Busch Stadium Improvements
Calfee Park Renovation
California State University-San Bernardino
Health and Physical Education Facility
Canal Park
Candlestick Park (3 Com Park)
Improvements
Carleton University Student
Recreation Center
Chelsea Football Club North Stand
Cheltenham Racecourse
Chicago Fire Temporary Stadium
Cincinnati Convention Center Renovation
Citizens Bank Park
City of Palms Park
Clemson University Kingsmore Stadium
Renovation
Clemson University LittleJohn Coliseum
Improvements
Cleveland Browns Stadium
Cleveland Browns Training Facility
Coca Cola All Star Park
College of William and Mary
Baseball Stadium
College of William and Mary Football
Training Facility
College of William and Mary Zable
Stadium Improvements
Colorado Springs World Arena
Comerica Park
Coors Field
Cotton Bowl Renovation
Croke Park Stadium
Dodgertown Spring Training Facility
Dunn Tire Park
Dunn Tire Park Improvements
Durham Bulls Athletic Park
E Center
Eastern Illinois University O'Brien Stadium
Turf Replacement
Ed Smith Sports Complex
Eden Park Extension

Edgbaston Cricket Grounds
Edison International Field
Edison International Field Club Improvements
Edward A. LeLacheur Park
Edward Jones Dome
Ericsson Stadium
Faro Stadium
FedExField
Fifth Third Field Expansion
First American Bank Ballpark at Scharbauer
Sports Complex
Florida State University Dick Howser
Stadium
Florida Suncoast Dome
Fort Worth Convention Center Expansion
Franklin Covey Field
Gaylord Entertainment Center
Georgia Tech Bobby Dodd Stadium
Expansion
Georgia Tech Russ Chandler Stadium
Giant Center
Giants Stadium Suite Additions
Gillette Stadium
Grand River Center
Grande Communications Football/Soccer
Stadium
Great American Ballpark
Great Leighs Racecourse
Greer Stadium Improvements
Grizzlies Stadium
HallamFM Arena
Harbor Park
Heinz Field
Hohokam Stadium
Homestead Spring Training Facility
Hong Kong Stadium
Hoover Metropolitan Stadium
Indiana Convention Center Expansion
Iowa Events Center
Iowa State University Ernst Lied
Recreation/Athletic Center
Ipswich Town Football Club North Stand
at Portman Road
Isotopes Park
Jacksonville Arena
Jacob Javits Convention Center
Jacobs Field
John O'Donnell Stadium Renovation
Joseph P. Riley Park
Kansas State University Frank Myers Field

Kansas State University Wagner
Field Expansion
Kauffman Stadium Renovation
Kean University Wellness Center/Athletic
Facility
Kempton Grandstand
Kennington Oval, Vauxhall End
King Alfred Sports Center
Knox College Fieldhouse Addition
Lake Terrace Convention Center
Lancaster Municipal Stadium
Lawrence Dumont Stadium Renovation
Leopardstown Racecourse
London Arena Renovation
Louisiana State University Tiger Stadium
Expansion
M&T Bank Stadium
Melbourne Cricket Ground Redevelopment
MGM Grand Conference Center
Miami Dolphins Training Facility
Mile High Stadium Suites Addition
Millennium Centre Redevelopment
Millennium Dome Arena
Millennium Stadium
Milton Keynes Stadium
Minute Maid Park
Montgomery Baseball Stadium
Nagano Olympic Oval
Nanjing Olympic Sports Centre
National Cycling Center
National Indoor Arena
Nelson Wolff Stadium
New Wembley Stadium
North Charleston Conference and
Performing Arts Center
Northern Illinois University Huskie
Stadium Expansion
Northern Kentucky Convention Center
Orange County Convention Center
Expansion
Oriole Park at Camden Yards
Osceola County Stadium
P&C Stadium
Pacific Bell Park
PaeTec Park
Palasport Speedskating Arena
Palmetto Exposition Center
Payson Field Renovation
Penang International Equestrian Centre
Penn State University Beaver
Stadium Expansion

Penn State University East Area Locker Room Renovation

Penn State University Louis E. Lasch Football Training Facility

Peoria Spring Training Facility

Pepsi Center

Petco Park

Philadelphia Phillies Spring Training Facility

Philip B. Elfstrom Stadium

Philips Arena

Phoenix Cardinals Stadium

Phoenix Civic Plaza Expansion

Phoenix Coyotes Arena

Pittsburgh Civic Arena Improvements

Plano Convention Center

PNC Park

Port St. Lucie Complex

Powerade Ieport

Pro Player Baseball Modifications

Pro Player Renovation

Pro Player Stadium

Raymond James Stadium

RCA Dome Renovation

Reebok Stadium

Reliant Stadium

Richmond County Bank Ballpark at St. George Station

Riverfront Stadium

Robin Park Athletics Arena

Roger Dean Stadium

Round Rock Athletic Complex

Royal Selangor Racecourse

Royals Crown Club at Kauffman Stadium

San Bernardino Stadium

San Diego State University Tony Gwynn Baseball Stadium

San Francisco 49ers Marie P DeBartolo Sports Center

San Francisco State University Student Physical Activities Center

Scottsdale Stadium

Sec Taylor Stadium

Senator Thomas J. Dodd Memorial Stadium

Shenzhen Pool

Solider Field Suite Addition

Springfield Exposition Center

St. Louis Cardinals Stadium

Stanley Coveleski Regional Stadium

Suffolk County Community College Brookhaven Gym

Suncorp Stadium

Super Bowl XIX

Super Bowl XIX/Stanford Stadium Modifications

Super Bowl XXII

Super Bowl XXII/Jack Murphy Stadium Modifications

Super Bowl XXXVII

Super Bowl XXXVIII

Surprise Recreation Complex

T.R. Hughes Ballpark

Taipei Arena

Tampa Convention Center

Tattersalls Stand at Cheltenham Racecourse

Telstra Dome

Telstra Stadium

Tempe Diablo Stadium

Texas A&M University Recreation Center

The Alamodome

The Baseball Grounds of Jacksonville

The Coliseum

The Evansville Centre

The Lansing Center

Three Rivers Stadium Improvements

Toulouse Stadium Renovation

Toyota Center

Tropicana Field

Troy State University Memorial Stadium Expansion

Tucson Electric Park

Tulane University Reily Recreation Center

Tulane University Wilson Athletic Center

U.S. Cellular Field

United Center

University of Arkansas Frank Baum Baseball Stadium

University of Buffalo World University Games Stadium

University of Connecticut Gampel Pavilion Renovation

University of Connecticut Multipurpose Training Facility

University of Delaware Bob Carpenter Center

University of Florida Ben Hill Griffin Carpenter Center

University of Florida Stephen C. O'Connell Center Stadium Expansion

University of Houston Athletics/Alumni Center Renovation

University of Kansas Allen Fieldhouse Renovation

University of Kansas Anderson Family Strength and Conditioning Center

University of Kansas Memorial Stadium Renovation and Pressbox Addition

University of Maryland Byrd Stadium Improvements

University of Maryland Football Team Building

University of Miami Mark Light Stadium

University of Michigan Stadium Renovation

University of Missouri Basketball Lounge

University of Missouri New Arena

University of Missouri Stadium Turf Replacement

University of New Mexico Endzone Building

University of New Mexico Training Facility

University of North Carolina at Greensboro War Memorial Stadium

University of Oklahoma Barry Switzer Center

University of Oklahoma Gaylord Family Memorial Stadium Improvements

University of Rhode Island Boss Arena

University of Rhode Island Thomas M. Ryan Center

University of South Florida Recreation Center

University of the Pacific Athletic Training Facility

University of Tulsa Donald W. Reynolds Center

University of Virginia McCue Football Training Center

University of West Florida Student Recreation Center

University of Wisconsin Kohl Center

University of Wisconsin-Milwaukee Klotsche Center

Verizon Wireless Arena

Veterans Stadium Concession Improvements

Victoria State Hockey and Netball Centre

Victory Field

Virginia Beach Soccer Stadium

Virginia Tech Lane Stadium South Endzone Expansion

Virginia Tech Lane Stadium West Sideline Expansion

Western Illinois University Student Recreation Center

Western Kentucky University Diddle Arena Renovation

Westpac Stadium

Wichita State University Charles Koch Arena

Wright State University Ervin J. Nutter Center Expansion and Renovation

Wrigley Field Improvements

Xcel Energy Center

XIX Olympic Winter Games (Salt Lake City)

XVIII Olympic Winter Games (Nagano)

XXIX Olympic Summer Games Study for New York, New York

XXVI Olympic Summer Games (Atlanta)

XXVI Olympic Summer Games Bid for Manchester, England

XXVI Olympic Summer Games Bid for San Francisco, California

XXVII Olympic Summer Games (Sydney)

XXX Olympic Summer Games Bid for London, England

XXX Olympic Summer Games Bid for New York City, New York

Zephyrs Field

Studies, Master Plans and Consultations

Air Canada Centre Design Consultation
Albany Convention Center Site Study
Alex George Park Design
Arco Park Conversion Study
Arlington Park Racetrack Study
Asheville Stadium Master Plan Study
Astrodome Conversion Study, Houston
Astrodome Master Plan Study
Livestock Show and Rodeo
Atlanta Braves Stadium Study
Auburn University Jordan-Hare Stadium
Master Plan
Auckland Arena Study and Master Plan
Augusta Civic Center Master Plan
Augusta, Georgia Ballpark Study
Augustana College Athletic Facilities
Improvements Plan
Austin, Texas Stadium Study
Bakersfield Baseball Stadium Master Plan
Ballpark Stadium Master Plan
Baltimore Orioles Spring Training
Facility Study
Bangkok Arena Study
Bangor Auditorium Study
Battery Park City Playing Field Study
Beckley Minor League Baseball Study
Beijing Olympic Master Plan
Beloit, Wisconsin Brewers Master Plan
Billings Minor League Ballpark Study
Birmingham Convention Center Complex
Master Plan
Birmingham Multipurpose Facility Study
Blockbuster Baseball Stadium Study
Bowling Green State University Arena
Design Study
Bridgewater State College Fieldhouse Study
Bristol Stadium Study
Buffalo Memorial Auditorium Renovation
and Master Plan
Calgary Olympic Park Master Plan
California Lutheran University Baseball
Stadium Study
Canton Sportsplex Master Plan
Carisbrook Oval Master Plan
Centennial Garden Arena Study
Chandler, Arizona Stadium Study
Charlotte, North Carolina Baseball
Stadium Study
Chattanooga Stadium Master Plan
Chouteau Lake Development Master Plan
Cincinnati Nippert Stadium Study

Cincinnati Riverfront Stadium Study
Coe College K. Raymond Clark Racquet
Center Study
Colorado Rapids Major League Soccer Study
Colorado State University Stadium Study
Columbus Sports and Entertainment
Complex Study
Concordia University Multiuse Facility Study
Coral Springs Multipurpose Stadium Study
Country Club Plaza Tennis Master Plan
Cox Business Services Convention Center
Master Plan
Croke Park Stadium Master Plan
Dallas Cowboys Training Facility Consultation
Dallas Mavericks Feasibility Study
Darlington International Raceway Master Plan
Davenport Arena Study
Daytona Speedway Improvement Study
Delaware Stadium Study
Des Moines Menace Soccer Stadium Study
Desert Sun Stadium Improvements Study
Detroit Lions Silverdome Study
Disneyworld Sports Master Plan
Docklands London Stadium Study
Dubai Autodrome F1 Master Plan
Dublin Ohio Soccer Stadium Design
Duke University Cameron Indoor Stadium
Durham Bulls Office Building and Stadium
Improvements Study
Dusseldorf Arena Study
Edmonton Stadium Design Study
Edward Jones Dome Facility Needs Analysis
El Paso Arena Study
Erie Civic Center Study and Master Plan
Erie, Pennsylvania Baseball Master Plan
Everett Stadium Complex Master Plan
Facility Study
Fairfield County Arena Design
FedExField Hospitality Village Design
Flamengo Football Club Training
Facility Design
Fort Valley State University Physical Education
Building Consultation
Garden of Champions Development Plan
Garden State International Speedway Study
Gator Bowl Renovation Study
Genesis Center Arena Study
Georgetown University McDonough Hall
Giants Stadium Dome Study
Improvements Study

Graham Park Study
Grand Wayne Center Expansion Study
Great Falls Stadium Study
Greenville Sports and Convention Study
Guadalajara Baseball Stadium Study
H.H. Metrodome Capital Improvements Study
Hagerstown A Baseball/Municipal
Stadium Study
Hamburg Arena Master Plan
Hampton Roads Study
Hancock Stadium Master Plan
Hannover Arena Design
Harborside Convention Center and
Hotel Study
Harris County Natatorium Study
Heartland Park Design
Hoboken Arena Planning and Design
Hoosier Dome Baseball Study
Houston Astros Spring Training Facility
Site Study
Howard University Sportsplex Design and
Master Plan
Hutchinson Community College Gowans
Stadium Renovation Study
IMA Arena Design
Imperial College Sports Center Study
Indiana University Athletic Facilities
Master Plan
Indiana University Auxiliary Gym Design
Indiana University Baseball Stadium Study
Indiana University Field Hockey Facility Plan
Indiana University Student Athletic
Center Study
International Speedway Corporation Study
Iowa State University Athletic Field Study
Iowa State University Jack Trice Stadium
Expansion Study
Irish Rugby Football Union Stadium
Development Plan
Jackie Robinson Field Renovation Study
Jackson County Sports Complex Master Plan
Jefferson Parish Stadium Master Plan
Johnson County Kansas Wizards
Soccer Design
Kawasaki, Japan Arena Study
Keating Arena Site Study
Kemper Arena Improvements Study
Kentucky International Speedway Design
Kingdome Master Plan Study
Kingdome Super Bowl and Final Four Study
Kino Park Spring Training Facility Master Plan

Knoxville Stadium Site Study
Lake Elsinore Stadium/Amphitheater
Feasibility Study
Lake Placid Olympic Center Arena
Lancaster Park Redevelopment Plan
Master Plan
Lander University Physical Fitness
Center Study
Lansing Michigan Baseball Master Plan
Las Vegas Arena Study
Las Vegas Stadium Study
Lexington, Kentucky Thoroughbred Study
Liberty Bowl Memorial Stadium Study
Little Fenway Youth Baseball Study
Liverpool Arena Renovation Study
London Arena Modification Study
Los Angeles Coliseum Modifications Study
Los Angeles Dodger's Spring Training
Facility Study
Los Angeles Sports Arena Study
Louisiana State University Alex Box
Stadium Study
Louisiana State University Tiger Stadium
Master Plan
LTA Training Centre Study
Macon Arena and Ballpark Study
Manners Park Conceptual Design Study
McCormick Field Master Plan
McCoy Stadium Renovation Study
McNichols Arena Improvements Study
Meadowlands Sports Complex Master Plan
MECCA Arena Study
Memphis Downs Racetrack Design
Mexico City Arena Study
Miami Heat Arena Study
Milwaukee Brewers Stadium Design Study
Minnesota Twins Ballpark Design
Modesto A Baseball Study
Montreal Expos New Stadium Study
Mount Clemens Minor League Baseball Study
Mount Vernon Arena Study
Munich Stadium Concept
Nassau Veterans Memorial Coliseum Study
Navy Marine Corps Memorial Stadium
Improvements Study
Needles, California Training Facility Study
New Castle County Stadium Study
New Mexico State University Pan American
Center Study
New York Islanders Arena Master Plan
New York Mets Ballpark Design

New York Sportsplex Study
New York Yankees Ballpark Design
New York/Trump Stadium Study
Newark Arena Study
Nigeria Baseball Technical Consulting
Norfolk Arena Study
North Carolina State University Baseball
  Stadium Expansion Study
Northern Arizona University Arena Plan
Northern Illinois University Arena
  Feasibility Study
Northern Virginia Baseball Site Selection
Notre Dame University Joyce Center Study
Oakland Arena Study
Oakland Athletics Site Study
Oakland Coliseum Capital Improvements Plan
Oakland Raiders Training Facility Study
Oakwell Master Plan Study
Ohio State University Athletic Facilities
  Master Plan
Onondaga County Multi-Use Stadium Study
Orange Bowl Renovation Study
Orange County Baseball Study
Orlando Arena Study
Owensboro Sports Center Study
Palasport Milano Arena Study
Palm Springs Spring Training Facility Master
  Plan Study
Palma Nova-Mallorca Spain Study
Parramatta Stadium Master Plan
Penn State University Arena Study
Penn State University Beaver Intercollegiate
  Athletic Facility Needs Study
Penn State University Beaver Stadium
  Improvements and Expansion Study
Peoria Chiefs Stadium Study
Phoenix Municipal Spring Training
  Facility Study
Phoenix Sports Complex Study
Pittsburgh Civic Arena Study
Pittsburgh North Shore Redevelopment Plan
Pittsfield Stadium Site Study
Plant City Softball Complex Study
PNC Park Adjacent Development Study
Point Stadium Improvements
Pontiac Silverdome Capital Improvements
  Study
Portland Baseball Stadium Study
Portland Tennis Stadium Study
Prospect Heights Arena Study
Providence Rhode Island Stadium Study
Ramapo College of New Jersey Recreation
  Center Improvements Plan
Ray Winder Field Renovation Study
Raymond James Stadium Study
Reno Minor League Baseball Study
Reno Recreation Center Study
Renton Arena Study

RFK Stadium Suite Renovation Study
Rockford Baseball Study
Rose Bowl Renovation Study
Round Rock Multi-Purpose Stadium Study
Sacramento Entertainment Complex Study
Saint Louis University Events Center/Grand
  Center Study
Salt Lake City Utah AAA Master Plan
San Bernardino Stadium Study
San Diego Chargers Master Plan
San Diego Chargers Training Facility
San Jose Silicon Valley Sports and Recreation
  Complex Master Plan
San Jose State University Spartan Stadium
  Improvements Study
Sarasota Arena Study
Sarasota Spring Training Facility Study
Scottish National Stadium Study
Seattle Kingdome Master Plan
Southern Connecticut State Baseball
  Field Study
Southern Illinois University Arena Floor
  Feasibility Study
Southern Illinois University McAndrew
  Stadium Improvement Study
Southwest Baseball Instructional Training
  Complex Study
Southwestern Bell Park-Oklahoma City
  Redhawks Ballpark Study
Spectrum Arena Expansion Study
Springfield Arena Study
Springfield Ballpark Study
St. Louis Gardens Arena Study
Stadivarios Arena Design
Stamford Arena Study
Stanford University Maples Pavilion
  Expansion Study
State of Connecticut Stadium Feasibility Study
Stockton Ports North Site Study
Sunderland Stadium Study
Syrcruse University Carrier Dome Study
Taipei Asian Games Study
Tallahassee Arena Study
Temple University Recreation and
  Convocation Center Study
Texas Motor Speedway Plan
Texas Stadium Improvements Study
Texas Tech Athletic Program Master Plan
The Alamodome Study
The Citadel Johnson Hagood Stadium
  Master Plan
The Lansing Center Master Plan
The Londondome Design
Three Rivers Stadium Suite Addition Study
Toledo Mudhens Site Study
Toronto Maple Leafs Garden Arena Study
Toronto Raptors Arena Design Study
Tucson Electric Park Master Plan

U.S. Military Academy Gillis Fieldhouse
  Rehabilitation Study
U.S. Naval Academy Memorial Stadium
  Renovation Masterplan
U.S. Naval Academy, Memorial Stadium
  Master Plan
U.S. Tennis Association Study
University of Alabama Athletic Facilities
  Master Plan
University of Arkansas War Memorial
  Stadium Renovation Master Plan
University of Cincinnati Athletics and
  Recreational Master Plan Study
University of Cincinnati Myrl Shoemaker
  Center Improvements Study
University of Connecticut Basketball
  Expansion Study
University of Florida Sports and Recreation
  Programming Study
University of Georgia Physical Activities
  Center Master Plan
University of Iowa Kinnick Stadium
  Expansion Study
University of Kansas Athletic Facilities
  Master Plan
University of Kansas Softball Study
University of Kansas Track and Field and
  Soccer Complex Study
University of Kentucky Rupp Arena
  Improvements Consulting
University of Maryland Arena/Union Study
University of Maryland Athletic and
  Recreation Master Plan
University of Maryland Byrd Stadium
  Expansion Study
University of Maryland Cole Field House
  Expansion Study
University of Miami Convocation Center
  Design Study
University of Minnesota Arena Design Study
University of Mississippi Vaught-Hemingway
  Stadium Expansion Master Plan
University of Missouri Athletic Facilities
  Master Plan
University of Nebraska Athletic Facilities
  Master Plan Study
University of Nebraska Skybox
  Programming Study
University of Nebraska Stadium
  Improvements Master Plan
University of Notre Dame Joyce Center
  Improvements Plan
University of Oklahoma Athletic Facilities
  Master Plan
University of Pittsburgh Athletic Facilities
  Master Plan
University of Pittsburgh Charles L. Cost
  Indoor Sports Facility Study

University of Rhode Island Football Stadium
  Master Plan
University of Southern California
  Arena Study
University of Tulsa Recreation Center Study
University of Virginia Athletic Facilities
  Master Plan
University of Virginia Indoor Practice
  Facility Study
University of Wisconsin-Green Bay Arena
  Programming Study
University of Wisconsin-Madison Athletic
  Facilities Study
Veterans Stadium Improvements Study
Virginia Beach Baseball Stadium Study
Virginia Tech Lane Stadium Expansion
  and Renovation Study
War Memorial Recreational Park
  Re-use Study
West Palm Beach Spring Training
  Facility Study
West Palm Beach Stadium Complex
  Master Plan
West Virginia State College Sports
  Master Plan
Western Kentucky University Arena Study
Wichita State University Athletic Facilities
  Master Plan
Wichita State University Levitt Arena
  Expansion Study
Wichita Wranglers Master Plan
Willimantic, Connecticut Baseball Study
Wilmington Stadium Design Study
Winnipeg, Canada Facility Study
Winston-Salem Baseball Stadium
  Master Plan Study
World Cup Soccer Arrowhead
  Stadium Study
World Cup Soccer Giants Stadium Study
Wright State University Athletic Facilities
  Master Plan
Wright State University Ervin J. Nutter
  Center Expansion Study
Wrigley Field Master Plan
Wyandotte County Kansas Race Track
  Master Plan
Yuma, Arizona Spring Training Master Plan
Zephyr Stadium Study

Photography

3rd FIFA Women's World Cup
John Todd/Digital Sports Archive 181

15th FIFA World Cup
David Madison 138

Super Bowl XXXVII
Chris Hagerty/Ridgeway International 139

XIX Olympic Winter Games
David Madison 146, 147
Mckeely, Pigott & Fox, enhancement by McConnell Graphics, photo by Dean Dixon 176
Bob Greenspon 177, 179

XXVII Olympic Summer Games
David Madison 147
reprinted with permission from the United States Olympic Committee

XXXVII Olympic Summer Games
David Madison 180

Alfred McAlpine Stadium
Ian Lawson 34

Alltel Stadium
Stephan O'Brien/Aero-Pic, Inc. 28
Larry Arnato/Creative Photographic Service 29

America's Center
Brian Kuhlmann 101

Anaheim Convention Center Expansion
Timothy Hursley 130, 132, 133, 134-135

Arrowhead Pond of Anaheim
John Sutton/John Sutton Photography 86

AutoZone Park
Mark J. Isvranko 160

Bradley Center
Howard N. Kaplan/HNK Architectural Photography, Inc. 32, 33

Canal Park
Jim Maguire/Maguire Photographics (left) 183
Dave Morris/City of Akron (right) 183

Cheltenham Racecourse
Richard Sowersby 35

City of Palms Park
Aerial Visions, Inc. 100

Cleveland Browns Stadium
Jim Maguire/Maguire Photographics 22, 23

Comerica Park
Justin Maconochie/Hedrich Blessing 192, 193

Coors Field
HOK Sport + Venue + Event 30
Thorney Liebemann 184, 185, 187
Patrick Bingham-Hall 186

Dunn Tire Park
Patricia Layman Bazelon 9, 26, 27

Durham Bulls Athletic Park
Jerry Markatos/Markatos Photography (top) 24
Tim Buchman/Tim Buchman Photography (bottom) 24

Edison International Field
Paul Bielenberg 112
The Lovero Group 113

Ericsson Stadium
Carolina Photo Group 162, 163

FedExField
Maxwell MacKenzie 42, 43

Fort Worth Convention Center Expansion
Craig Blackmon, AIA 129

Franklin Covey Field
Scot Zimmerman Architectural Photography 25

Gaylord Entertainment Center
Michael Lewis 13, 178

Georgia Tech Bobby Dodd Stadium
John Lucarini/HOK Sport + Venue + Event 172

Giant Center
Ed Massery/Massery Photography 98

Gillette Stadium
Patrick Bingham-Hall 148, 149

Great American Ball Park
Jim Maguire/Maguire Photographics 94, 95, 96, 97
Patrick Bingham-Hall 58
J. Miles Wolf/Wolf Photographic Arts 59

Grizzlies Stadium
Daron Bennett 99

Hallam FM Arena
Steve Place/Lloyd Photography 72

Harbor Park
MacGregor Enterprises 56

Heinz Field
Patrick Bingham-Hall 154, 155, 156
Jim Schafer (top) 157
Ed Massery/Massery Photography (bottom) 157

Hohokam Stadium
Phil Masters 52

Homestead Sports Complex
George Cott/Chroma, Inc. 87

Hong Kong Stadium
Kenzi Ip/Ling's Workshop 12, 76, 77, 78, 79

Indiana Convention Center Expansion
Timothy Hursley 152

Isotopes Park
Robert Reck 161

Jacobs Field
Timothy Hursley 13, 18, 19, 20-21
HOK Sport + Venue + Event 74

John O'Donnell Stadium Renovation
Robert Boyd 164

Joseph P. Riley, Jr Park
Dickson Dunlap 110

Kansas State University Wagner Field Expansion
Todd Feeback 175

M&T Bank Stadium
Maxwell MacKenzie 108, 109

Mile High Stadium Suites
Bill Mathis 57

Millennium Stadium
Patrick Bingham-Hall 36, 37, 38, 39

Minute Maid Park
Rion Rizzo/Creative Sources Photography, Inc. 124
Patrick Bingham-Hall 125
Mark Green/Mark Green Photography 126-127

The Alamodome
Greg Hursley/Greg Hursley, Inc. 54
Scott McDonald/Hedrich Blessing 55

National Indoor Arena
Lloyd Photography 73

The Baseball Grounds of Jacksonville
Will Dickey 136

The E Center
Scot Zimmerman Architectural Photography 92

The Mane P DeBartolo Sports Center
Russell Abraham 128

The United Center
George Lambros Photography 68, 69, 88
Assassi Productions 60

Pacific Bell Park
Patrick Bingham-Hall 6, 195, 196-197

Oriole Park at Camden Yards
Jeff Goldberg/Esto Photographics 11, 46, 62, 64, 65
Patrick Bingham-Hall 63, 66-67

Pepsi Center
Thorney Liebemann 166, 167, 169
Jodee Shumaker 168

Penn State University Beaver Stadium Expansion
Jim Maguire/Maguire Photographics 122

Penn State University Louis E. Lasch Training Facility
Ed Massery/Massery Photography 93

Nanjing Olympic Sports Centre
HOK Sport + Venue + Event 17

Philips Arena
Rion Rizzo/Creative Sources Photography, Inc. 90, 91

Phoenix Civic Plaza Expansion
HOK Sport + Venue + Event 16

Pittsburgh Riverfront Master Plan
HOK Sport + Venue + Event 116

PNC Park
Ed Massery/Massery Photography 82, 83, 84, (bottom) 85
Jim Schafer (top) 85

Pro Player Stadium
George Cott/Chroma, Inc. 80, 81
Smith Aerial Photography 9

Reebok Stadium
Ian Lawson 41

Reliant Stadium
Patrick Bingham-Hall 118, 119, 120, 158
Mark Green/Mark Green Photography (top) 121
Ed Massery/Massery Photography (bottom) 121

Richmond County Bank Ballpark at St. George Station
Maxwell MacKenzie 114, 115

Roger Dean Stadium
George Cott/Chroma, Inc. 111

Scottsdale Stadium
Bob Freund/Craig Smith 151

Stamford Bridge North Stand
Ian Lawson 123

Surprise Recreation Campus
Bill Sperry 150

Suncorp Stadium
Patrick Bingham-Hall 48, 49, 50, 51, 102

Telstra Dome
David B Simmonds 104
Patrick Bingham-Hall 105, 106, 107

Telstra Stadium
Patrick Bingham-Hall 14, 140, 141, 142, 143, 144
reprinted with permission from the United States Olympic Committee 141

University of Arkansas Baum Stadium at George Cole Field
Elliot Neel 44

University of Delaware Bob Carpenter Convocation Center
Alan Karchmer 182

University of Houston Athletics and Alumni Center
Richard Payne 171

University of Kansas Anderson Family Strength and Conditioning Center
Daron Bennett 170

University of Rhode Island The Thomas M. Ryan Center
Frank Giuliani 165

University of Tulsa Donald W. Reynolds Center
Howard N. Kaplan/HNK Architectural Photography, Inc. 174

University of Wisconsin The Kohl Center
Ed Purcell 40

Virginia Tech Lane Stadium Expansion
Ben Standl/HOK Sport + Venue + Event 137

Victory Field
John Bragg/Power Images 45

Wembley Stadium
GMJ Design Ltd 16

Westpac Stadium
Patrick Bingham-Hall 190, 191

Wrigley Field Improvements
Stephen Green Photography 153

Xcel Energy Center
Bob Perzel 70, 71

Acknowledgements

Advisory Committee: Bradd Crowley, Debbie Frederiksen, Phil Holstra, Erin Hubert, Erin Jones, Jon Knight, Rick Martin, Carrie Plummer, Earl Santee, John Shreve

Principal: Earl Santee

Text and Overall Coordination: Carrie Plummer

Details Coordination: Erin Jones

Image Coordination: Erin Hubert

Transcription: Kyleen Miller, Mellaine Burris, Tina Diaz, Kathy Elevier, Joan Hammes, Monica Hollis, Sherri Robinson, Becca Sherer, Joan Stout

Additional Assistance: Michele Fleming, Wes Heaton, Phil Holstra, Tracy Parsons, Kristi Pospichal, Bob White, Barbara Cronn